Weathering the Seasons

Weathering the Seasons

Matthew Petchinsky

Weathering the Seasons: Groundhog Day Perspectives
By: Matthew Petchinsky

Introduction: How Groundhog Day Traditions Teach Us About Resilience

Groundhog Day is more than a whimsical tradition of watching a small, furry animal predict the weather; it is a profound metaphor for the cycles of life and the resilience required to navigate them. Each year on February 2nd, communities across North America gather to celebrate this unique occasion, blending folklore, community spirit, and a touch of hope as they look to the groundhog for signs of what lies ahead. Beyond its charming surface, Groundhog Day holds timeless lessons in perseverance, adaptability, and the strength of human spirit.

At its core, Groundhog Day reflects humanity's enduring relationship with nature and our ability to find meaning in its patterns. The ritual, rooted in ancient traditions like Candlemas Day and the German superstition about hedgehogs, reveals a deep-seated human need to connect with seasonal changes and prepare for the challenges they bring. The groundhog's prediction—whether for six more weeks of winter or the early arrival of spring—symbolizes the uncertainties of life. In this annual moment of suspense, we are reminded of our capacity to embrace unpredictability with both patience and optimism.

Resilience is the ability to adapt and thrive amid change, and Groundhog Day serves as an allegory for this essential quality. Just as the seasons transition in their unyielding rhythm, so do the circumstances of our lives. The groundhog's emergence from its burrow mirrors the courage it takes to confront life's trials head-on, while its retreat into the shadows reflects the wisdom of sometimes stepping back to reassess and recharge. Both responses are valid, and together, they demonstrate the balance necessary for enduring hardship and achieving personal growth.

The celebration of Groundhog Day also underscores the importance of community in fostering resilience. From Punxsutawney, Pennsylvania, to small towns across the continent, people come together to share in this tradition, bridging gaps between generations, neighbors, and even strangers. These gatherings remind us that resilience is not a solitary pursuit; it is built upon shared experiences, mutual support, and collective hope. The festivities, complete with music, laughter, and storytelling, transform the somber reality of a lingering winter into a joyous event that binds communities in the face of adversity.

Furthermore, the concept of repeating cycles, so emblematic of Groundhog Day, is a poignant reminder of the lessons life continually offers us. Whether viewed through the lens of personal setbacks or broader societal challenges, the "reset button" embodied by Groundhog Day encourages us to approach each new opportunity with renewed determination. In its repetitive nature, the tradition speaks to the human capacity to learn, grow, and ultimately break free from patterns that no longer serve us—a powerful message for building resilience.

In this introduction, we begin to uncover how Groundhog Day's blend of folklore, humor, and hope offers a roadmap for resilience. By delving deeper into its origins, traditions, and symbolism, we can draw practical insights for navigating the complexities of modern life. Whether the groundhog sees its shadow or not, the lessons of this time-honored tradition remain constant: resilience is about facing the cold realities of winter with the belief that spring will inevitably come.

Chapter 1: The Groundhog as a Weather Predictor

Groundhog Day is most famously associated with a groundhog emerging from its burrow to predict the arrival of spring or the continuation of winter. This whimsical weather forecasting tradition has captured the imagination of millions, blending folklore with the natural rhythms of the seasons. But how did a groundhog—an otherwise ordinary rodent—become the centerpiece of such a celebrated ritual? To understand the role of the groundhog as a weather predictor, we must explore its cultural origins, its biological behaviors, and the intricate symbolism that has elevated this humble creature to the status of meteorological icon.

Historical Origins of the Groundhog as a Weather Forecaster

The tradition of Groundhog Day has its roots in ancient European customs, particularly those linked to Candlemas Day, a Christian holiday observed on February 2nd. Candlemas itself evolved from earlier pagan festivals celebrating the midpoint between the winter solstice and the spring equinox, a time of year that carried significant agricultural and spiritual importance. On Candlemas, clergy would bless and distribute candles, symbolizing light and hope for the remaining winter days.

A key part of Candlemas lore involved weather forecasting. According to an old English rhyme:

If Candlemas Day be fair and bright,
Winter will have another fight.
If Candlemas Day brings cloud and rain,
Winter won't come again.

This superstition crossed the English Channel to Germany, where the weather-predicting role was assigned to animals—particularly hedgehogs or badgers. German immigrants brought this tradition to North America in the 18th and 19th centuries, where they adapted it to the local wildlife. The groundhog, or woodchuck, became the chosen animal due to its hibernation habits and abundance in the region, particularly in Pennsylvania.

The Biology Behind the Groundhog's Behavior

To appreciate the groundhog as a weather predictor, it's essential to understand its biological characteristics. Groundhogs (Marmota monax) are members of the marmot family, known for their burrowing habits and deep hibernation cycles. As a true hibernator, the groundhog undergoes significant physiological changes during the winter months, including a dramatic reduction in heart rate, body temperature, and metabolic activity. These adaptations allow it to conserve energy while surviving harsh winter conditions.

Groundhogs typically emerge from hibernation in early February, aligning with Groundhog Day festivities. However, their emergence is not influenced by a conscious effort to predict the weather. Instead, it is driven by biological imperatives, such as mating behaviors and environmental cues like increasing daylight. The tradition of the groundhog "seeing its shadow" likely arose from observations of this natural behavior, combined with the human tendency to assign symbolic meaning to seasonal changes.

Interpreting the Groundhog's Prediction

The folklore surrounding the groundhog's prediction is delightfully simple: if the groundhog sees its shadow upon emerging from its burrow, it retreats, signaling six more weeks of winter. If it does not see its shadow, spring is said to arrive early. While this tradition is more playful than scientific, it reflects humanity's enduring fascination with nature's ability to provide clues about the future.

From a meteorological perspective, the groundhog's predictions have a mixed record of accuracy. Studies suggest that Punxsutawney Phil, the most famous groundhog in the United States, has an accuracy rate of around 39%, well below the standard for modern weather forecasting. Despite this, the charm of the ritual lies not in its precision but in its symbolic representation of hope and anticipation.

The Groundhog as a Symbol

The groundhog's role as a weather predictor extends beyond its biological behaviors. It has become a cultural symbol of renewal, resilience, and the cyclical nature of life. Emerging from its burrow each February, the groundhog reminds us of the delicate balance between dormancy and activity, rest and renewal. Its moment in the spotlight offers a break from winter's monotony and serves as a communal celebration of perseverance through the colder months.

Moreover, the groundhog's emergence highlights humanity's reliance on nature for guidance and inspiration. Long before advanced meteorological tools, people looked to animals, plants, and celestial patterns to interpret the world around them. The groundhog, with its predictable hibernation cycle, became an accessible and relatable figure in this age-old tradition of natural observation.

The Evolution of Groundhog Day

The groundhog's status as a weather predictor was cemented in 1887 with the first official Groundhog Day celebration in Punxsutawney, Pennsylvania. Organized by the Punxsutawney Groundhog Club, this event elevated the groundhog from a regional curiosity to a national phenomenon. Over the decades, the celebration has grown into a highly anticipated spectacle, complete with ceremonies, media coverage, and the playful participation of "Punxsutawney Phil."

In the years since its inception, Groundhog Day has transcended its roots to become a broader cultural event. The tradition has inspired festivals, parades, and even a beloved Hollywood film, cementing the groundhog's role as an enduring figure of folklore and entertainment.

Conclusion

The groundhog as a weather predictor embodies a unique blend of science, folklore, and cultural tradition. While its accuracy as a meteorological forecaster may be questionable, its significance as a symbol of seasonal change and resilience is undeniable. Through its annual emergence, the groundhog invites us to reflect on the rhythms of nature and the timeless human desire to find meaning in its patterns. In celebrating the groundhog, we celebrate the hope of renewal and the promise of brighter days ahead—a lesson that resonates far beyond the burrow.

Chapter 2: Lessons from Seasonal Transitions

Seasonal transitions are among nature's most profound teachers, offering lessons in adaptation, resilience, and the cyclical nature of life. These shifts, whether from winter to spring, summer to autumn, or any point in between, serve as powerful reminders of the inevitability of change and the opportunities it brings. Groundhog Day, occurring at the midpoint between the winter solstice and spring equinox, sits at a symbolic crossroads where the harshness of winter begins to give way to the promise of renewal. By examining the lessons embedded in these seasonal transitions, we can uncover valuable insights into how to navigate life's uncertainties and transformations.

1. The Wisdom of Patience

Winter, with its dormant fields and icy landscapes, teaches us the value of patience. Just as the earth rests and conserves its energy during this time, so too must we learn to pause and reflect during periods of stagnation or hardship. Groundhog Day, situated in the heart of winter, reminds us that change is often slow and deliberate. Whether the groundhog sees its shadow or not, the arrival of spring is inevitable—it is merely a matter of timing.

Patience is not passive; it is an active choice to endure and prepare. Farmers, for example, use the winter months to plan crops, repair tools, and gather resources, knowing that their preparations will bear fruit in the coming seasons. Similarly, we can use life's "winters" to nurture our goals, develop skills, and ready ourselves for opportunities that lie ahead.

2. The Importance of Adaptability

As seasons change, adaptability becomes essential for survival. Animals adjust their behaviors, migrating, hibernating, or foraging differently depending on the time of year. Plants, too, respond to seasonal cues, shedding leaves in autumn, conserving resources in winter, and blooming anew in spring. These natural responses demonstrate the importance of flexibility and responsiveness to external conditions.

Groundhog Day encapsulates this lesson through its playful weather prediction. Whether winter persists or spring arrives early, the message is clear: we must adapt to whatever comes our way. In life, adaptability allows us to pivot in the face of unexpected challenges and seize new opportunities, transforming obstacles into stepping stones for growth.

3. Resilience in the Face of Hardship

Winter often symbolizes hardship, with its scarcity of resources and harsh conditions. Yet even in the bleakest moments, nature demonstrates remarkable resilience. Trees survive freezing temperatures by drawing nutrients inward, animals grow thicker coats or store fat, and seeds lie dormant beneath the snow, waiting for the warmth of spring to awaken them.

The groundhog's emergence from its burrow mirrors this resilience. Whether it faces a cloudy sky or its own shadow, it reemerges year after year, undeterred by the uncertainty of the outcome. This resilience teaches us to face challenges with courage and determination, knowing that, like the seasons, difficulties are temporary and will eventually give way to brighter days.

4. The Cyclical Nature of Life

Seasonal transitions highlight the cyclical nature of life, where every end is also a beginning. Winter's dormancy gives way to spring's renewal, which blossoms into summer's abundance before fading into autumn's harvest. This constant cycle reminds us that life is not a straight path but a series of recurring phases, each with its own purpose and value.

Groundhog Day's placement at the midpoint of winter symbolizes this turning point, where the darkest days begin to give way to increasing light. It encourages us to view life's challenges as part of a larger journey, where setbacks are temporary and progress is always possible.

Understanding life as a cycle allows us to approach both successes and failures with a sense of perspective. Just as no winter lasts forever, no triumph is permanent. Embracing this ebb and flow fosters humility, gratitude, and the ability to weather life's ups and downs with grace.

5. The Value of Hope and Renewal

Spring's arrival, heralded by longer days and warmer temperatures, symbolizes renewal and the promise of growth. Groundhog Day captures this spirit of hope, offering a lighthearted reminder that even the coldest winters eventually thaw. The mere act of anticipating spring can lift spirits, encouraging communities to come together in celebration and shared optimism.

Hope is a powerful force that sustains us through adversity. It fuels our efforts, inspires creativity, and strengthens our resolve to overcome challenges. Seasonal transitions teach us that even when circumstances seem bleak, new opportunities and beginnings are just around the corner.

6. Alignment with Natural Rhythms

One of the most profound lessons from seasonal transitions is the importance of aligning ourselves with the natural world. Ancient cultures lived in harmony with the seasons, timing their agricultural, spiritual, and social activities to the rhythms of nature. Groundhog Day, with its origins in agricultural and pagan traditions, reflects this deep connection.

In modern life, we often lose sight of these rhythms, overwhelmed by the constant demands of technology and urbanization. Reconnecting with nature—by observing the seasons, celebrating traditions like Groundhog Day, or simply spending time outdoors—can ground us, reduce stress, and foster a sense of balance and well-being.

7. Community and Shared Traditions

Seasonal transitions have long been occasions for communal gatherings, as people come together to celebrate, share resources, and prepare for what lies ahead. Groundhog Day exemplifies this communal spirit, drawing crowds to small towns like Punxsutawney and inspiring celebrations across North America.

These shared traditions remind us that we are not alone in facing life's challenges. By supporting one another, exchanging wisdom, and celebrating milestones together, we strengthen the bonds that sustain us through life's seasons. Whether it's sharing laughter at a Groundhog Day festival or working together to navigate a difficult winter, community is an essential ingredient for resilience.

Conclusion

The lessons of seasonal transitions—patience, adaptability, resilience, the cyclical nature of life, hope, alignment with nature, and community—offer timeless guidance for navigating the complexities of human existence. Groundhog Day, situated at the heart of winter, serves as a symbolic touchpoint for these lessons, blending tradition, folklore, and seasonal wisdom into a celebration that resonates far beyond its playful premise.

By embracing the teachings of the seasons, we can cultivate the strength and flexibility needed to thrive in an ever-changing world. Whether we find ourselves in the depths of winter or on the cusp of spring, the cycles of nature remind us that change is both inevitable and essential, a source of growth, renewal, and boundless possibility.

Chapter 3: Preparing for the Unexpected

Life, like the weather, is full of unpredictability. Groundhog Day, with its playful focus on the groundhog's shadow as a harbinger of winter's persistence or spring's early arrival, is a lighthearted reminder that the future often refuses to be neatly packaged or forecasted. This unpredictability can be unsettling, but it also holds the key to resilience and growth. In this chapter, we will explore how the lessons of Groundhog Day can help us prepare for the unexpected, whether in weather, life, or the broader uncertainties of the world.

1. The Nature of Uncertainty

Uncertainty is an inherent part of life, woven into the fabric of our experiences. Groundhog Day, with its roots in weather prediction, mirrors this truth. Despite advances in meteorology, weather remains difficult to predict with perfect accuracy, just as life's twists and turns often defy our expectations. The groundhog's annual emergence underscores the duality of hope and unpredictability, reminding us that even the most well-laid plans can be disrupted by unforeseen events.

Acknowledging uncertainty is the first step in preparing for the unexpected. It allows us to approach life with humility, recognizing that control is often an illusion. While we cannot predict every storm or setback, we can cultivate the skills and mindset needed to weather them.

2. Building a Foundation of Resilience

Resilience is the ability to adapt and thrive in the face of adversity, and it is a critical skill for navigating uncertainty. Just as animals prepare for winter by gathering food and insulating their burrows, we can strengthen our capacity to face challenges by building a solid foundation of mental, emotional, and practical resilience.

- **Mental resilience** involves cultivating a growth mindset, which views challenges as opportunities for learning and development rather than insurmountable obstacles. This perspective enables us to approach uncertainty with curiosity and creativity.

- **Emotional resilience** is built through self-awareness and emotional regulation, allowing us to remain calm and focused in the face of unexpected stressors. Practices like mindfulness and journaling can help us process emotions constructively.
- **Practical resilience** involves proactive preparation for potential disruptions. From financial savings to emergency supplies, having tangible resources in place can provide stability during turbulent times.

Groundhog Day, with its themes of preparation and adaptability, invites us to reflect on how we can build resilience in our own lives. Whether through personal development, community support, or practical planning, resilience equips us to face uncertainty with confidence.

3. The Role of Preparation

Preparation is a powerful antidote to the anxiety of uncertainty. While we cannot predict every eventuality, we can anticipate potential scenarios and take steps to mitigate their impact. This principle is evident in nature, where animals and ecosystems exhibit remarkable strategies for coping with change.

The groundhog, for instance, exemplifies preparation through its hibernation cycle. By building fat reserves and constructing secure burrows, it ensures its survival during winter's scarcity. Similarly, ancient agrarian societies relied on careful planning and resource management to endure harsh seasons and uncertain harvests.

In our modern lives, preparation takes many forms:

- **Emergency planning:** Creating contingency plans for unexpected events, such as natural disasters, job loss, or health crises, can provide a sense of security and reduce the impact of disruptions.
- **Financial readiness:** Building an emergency fund and maintaining a budget are crucial for navigating economic uncertainties.

- **Skill development:** Learning new skills, whether practical (e.g., first aid) or professional (e.g., digital literacy), increases our adaptability and opens new opportunities.

Groundhog Day's celebration of seasonal change reminds us of the value of being prepared—not out of fear, but out of respect for life's inherent unpredictability.

4. Flexibility and Adaptability

Even the best preparations cannot account for every possibility. Flexibility and adaptability are essential qualities for thriving in the face of unexpected challenges. Just as the groundhog adjusts its behavior based on environmental conditions, we must be willing to pivot when circumstances change.

Adaptability requires a combination of openness, resourcefulness, and resilience:

- **Openness** involves embracing change as a natural part of life rather than resisting it. This mindset fosters a sense of adventure and creativity in responding to new situations.
- **Resourcefulness** is the ability to solve problems and find solutions with the tools and knowledge at hand. It is a skill that grows through practice and experience.
- **Resilience**, as discussed earlier, provides the emotional and mental fortitude needed to persevere through uncertainty.

Groundhog Day's dual outcomes—six more weeks of winter or an early spring—illustrate the importance of adaptability. Whether the weather turns harsh or mild, communities find ways to celebrate, demonstrating that flexibility is key to maintaining joy and purpose in unpredictable times.

5. Learning from Past Experiences

Preparing for the unexpected also involves learning from past experiences. History, both personal and collective, offers valuable insights into how to navigate uncertainty. Groundhog Day, with its roots in centuries-old traditions, reflects humanity's enduring efforts to find meaning and guidance in the patterns of nature.

By reflecting on our own experiences, we can identify lessons that inform future decisions:

- **Recognizing patterns:** Understanding the recurring cycles in our lives, whether financial, emotional, or social, helps us anticipate challenges and opportunities.
- **Evaluating outcomes:** Analyzing the successes and failures of past efforts allows us to refine our strategies and improve our responses to uncertainty.
- **Celebrating growth:** Acknowledging how we've overcome past challenges reinforces our confidence and resilience, empowering us to face new uncertainties with strength.

6. The Power of Community

One of the most enduring lessons of Groundhog Day is the importance of community in preparing for the unexpected. The celebration itself is a communal event, bringing people together to share in the joys and uncertainties of the season. This sense of connection is vital in times of unpredictability.

Communities provide support, resources, and collective wisdom that amplify individual resilience. From neighbors helping one another during storms to global networks collaborating on solutions to shared challenges, the power of community cannot be overstated. Building and nurturing these connections ensures that we are not alone when faced with life's uncertainties.

Conclusion

Preparing for the unexpected is a multifaceted endeavor that requires a blend of resilience, adaptability, preparation, and community. Groundhog Day, with its lighthearted approach to weather prediction, serves as a symbolic reminder that life is filled with uncertainties—and that this unpredictability can be met with courage, creativity, and hope.

By embracing the lessons of preparation, flexibility, and shared support, we can navigate the unknown with confidence. Whether winter lingers or spring arrives early, the key is to approach each moment with a readiness to adapt and a belief in our ability to thrive. In doing so, we honor the spirit of Groundhog Day and the timeless wisdom it imparts about resilience and renewal.

Chapter 4: The Interplay of Hope and Patience

Hope and patience are two of humanity's most enduring virtues, and their interplay creates a powerful foundation for navigating life's uncertainties and challenges. Groundhog Day, with its whimsical tradition of waiting for a groundhog's prediction, offers a metaphor for this delicate balance. Whether hoping for an early spring or patiently enduring a longer winter, this ritual reflects the universal experience of yearning for better days while understanding that some things take time to unfold. In this chapter, we will explore how hope and patience work together, their role in resilience and growth, and the profound lessons they teach us about the cycles of life.

1. Defining Hope and Patience

Hope is often described as the belief in a better future, the inner conviction that positive outcomes are possible despite present difficulties. It is a driving force that motivates action, inspires creativity, and sustains us through life's hardships. Hope, however, is not passive—it requires faith, courage, and a willingness to imagine possibilities beyond current circumstances.

Patience, on the other hand, is the ability to endure delays, challenges, or adversity without becoming discouraged. It is an active state of perseverance that allows us to stay grounded and focused, even when progress is slow or outcomes are uncertain. Patience is the counterpart to hope, providing the endurance needed to realize the vision hope inspires.

Together, hope and patience form a dynamic interplay. Hope provides the vision, while patience provides the strength to wait for its realization.

2. Lessons from Nature: The Patience of Seasons

Nature is a masterclass in the balance of hope and patience, particularly in the transitions between seasons. Winter, with its barrenness and cold, symbolizes a time of waiting and stillness. Yet beneath the surface, life persists—seeds lie dormant, animals conserve energy, and the earth quietly prepares for spring's renewal. The eventual arrival of spring is a testament to hope realized through patience.

Groundhog Day embodies this lesson. The groundhog's emergence symbolizes the hope of change, while the possibility of six more weeks of winter reminds us that patience is often required to see that hope fulfilled. This seasonal rhythm mirrors life's cycles, teaching us to trust the process and embrace both the anticipation of better days and the fortitude to endure the present.

3. The Role of Hope in Resilience

Hope is a cornerstone of resilience, providing the motivation to persist through difficulties and envision a brighter future. It allows individuals and communities to rise above setbacks, maintain perspective, and continue striving for their goals.

In the context of Groundhog Day, hope is evident in the collective anticipation of spring's arrival. This simple act of looking forward demonstrates how hope fosters positivity and connection, even in the face of uncertainty. Similarly, in our own lives, hope encourages us to:

- **Set goals:** Hope inspires us to define aspirations and work toward them.
- **Stay optimistic:** Believing in the possibility of improvement helps us maintain a positive outlook, even during challenging times.
- **Take action:** Hope motivates effort and persistence, driving us to seek solutions and opportunities.

However, hope without patience can lead to frustration and despair when outcomes are delayed. This is why the interplay of hope and patience is so crucial.

4. Patience as the Anchor

While hope provides the vision, patience anchors us in the present. It helps us manage expectations, cope with delays, and find contentment in the process rather than fixating solely on outcomes. Patience also fosters emotional stability, allowing us to approach challenges with a calm and measured perspective.

Groundhog Day's focus on seasonal change illustrates the necessity of patience. Whether spring arrives early or winter lingers, nature moves at its own pace, indifferent to human timelines. This teaches us the value of acceptance and the wisdom of aligning our expectations with the natural flow of life.

Developing patience involves:

- **Practicing mindfulness:** Focusing on the present moment reduces anxiety about the future.
- **Setting realistic expectations:** Understanding that progress takes time helps manage frustration.
- **Celebrating small victories:** Acknowledging incremental progress reinforces perseverance.

Through patience, we learn to appreciate the journey as much as the destination, finding meaning and growth in the waiting.

5. The Interplay of Hope and Patience in Action

The synergy between hope and patience is evident in many aspects of life, from personal growth to community resilience. When balanced effectively, these virtues create a powerful framework for overcoming adversity and achieving long-term goals.

- **Personal growth:** Hope motivates self-improvement, while patience allows for gradual progress. For example, learning a new skill requires the hope of mastery and the patience to practice consistently.
- **Relationships:** Hope sustains connections during difficult times, while patience fosters understanding and forgiveness, enabling relationships to endure and deepen.
- **Community resilience:** Hope unites communities in the face of shared challenges, while patience allows them to work steadily toward collective solutions.

Groundhog Day serves as a metaphor for this interplay, inviting us to hold onto hope while respecting the need for patience. Whether the groundhog predicts a long winter or an early spring, the message remains the same: transformation is a process that unfolds in its own time.

6. Cultivating Hope and Patience

Both hope and patience are skills that can be nurtured and strengthened through intentional practice. Groundhog Day offers a unique opportunity to reflect on these virtues and incorporate them into our lives.

- **Cultivating hope:**
    - Focus on possibilities rather than limitations.
    - Surround yourself with positive influences and supportive communities.
    - Set meaningful goals and break them into achievable steps.
    - Celebrate progress and milestones, no matter how small.
- **Cultivating patience:**
    - Practice mindfulness and gratitude to stay present.
    - Reframe delays as opportunities for growth or preparation.
    - Develop routines that promote consistency and stability.
    - Embrace the idea that setbacks are part of the journey.

By integrating hope and patience into our daily lives, we create a foundation for resilience and fulfillment, capable of weathering life's uncertainties with grace.

7. The Spiritual Dimension of Hope and Patience

For many, hope and patience hold a spiritual significance, representing trust in a higher power or the natural order of the universe. Groundhog Day, rooted in ancient traditions and seasonal rhythms, reflects this spiritual perspective. It reminds us that life operates on a timeline larger than our own and that faith in the process is essential for navigating the unknown.

This spiritual dimension encourages us to:

- Trust that challenges have purpose and meaning.
- Find comfort in the cycles of renewal and transformation.
- Recognize the interconnectedness of all things and our role within the greater whole.

Conclusion

The interplay of hope and patience is a profound lesson embedded in the traditions of Groundhog Day and the cycles of nature it celebrates. Together, these virtues provide the vision to dream of better days and the endurance to navigate the waiting. They remind us that life's challenges and uncertainties are not merely obstacles but opportunities for growth and transformation.

By embracing both hope and patience, we align ourselves with the natural rhythms of life, finding strength and meaning in the journey. Whether waiting for spring, working toward a goal, or enduring a difficult season, the balance of hope and patience ensures that we remain grounded, optimistic, and prepared for whatever lies ahead.

Chapter 5: Thriving Through Seasonal Changes

Seasonal changes are more than shifts in weather—they symbolize cycles of transformation, renewal, and opportunity. Whether transitioning from the depths of winter to the awakening of spring or moving from the vibrancy of summer to the reflective quiet of autumn, each season brings unique challenges and gifts. Thriving through these changes requires adaptability, mindfulness, and a proactive approach to making the most of what each season has to offer. Groundhog Day, with its focus on seasonal transition, provides a meaningful context to explore how we can not only endure but thrive through the changes in nature and life.

1. Understanding Seasonal Transitions

Seasons are nature's way of marking the passage of time and the cycles of life. They remind us that nothing is permanent and that each phase serves a purpose. These transitions often mirror our personal and collective experiences:

- **Winter:** A season of rest and reflection, winter encourages conservation of energy, introspection, and planning for the future.
- **Spring:** A time of renewal and growth, spring is associated with fresh beginnings, planting seeds (literally and metaphorically), and nurturing new ideas.
- **Summer:** A period of abundance and action, summer is marked by long days, energy, and the opportunity to bring plans to fruition.
- **Autumn:** A season of harvest and preparation, autumn invites reflection on achievements, gratitude, and readiness for the slower pace of winter.

Groundhog Day falls at the midpoint of winter, symbolizing the tension between enduring the present and anticipating the future. By embracing the lessons of each season, we can align ourselves with these natural rhythms and find ways to thrive through their transitions.

2. Embracing Change with Adaptability

Thriving through seasonal changes begins with adaptability—the ability to adjust our behaviors, mindsets, and expectations to meet the demands of each season. In nature, adaptability is a survival mechanism: animals hibernate, migrate, or grow thicker fur, while plants shed leaves or conserve resources. Similarly, humans must adapt to external changes while maintaining inner balance.

- **Physical adaptation:** Adjusting routines, clothing, and activities to suit seasonal conditions. For example, layering clothing in winter or staying hydrated in summer.
- **Mental adaptation:** Shifting goals and expectations to align with seasonal opportunities. Spring might inspire creativity, while winter encourages introspection.
- **Emotional adaptation:** Recognizing and managing the emotional effects of seasonal changes, such as the "winter blues" or the restlessness of spring fever.

Groundhog Day reminds us that adaptability is not about resisting change but embracing it. Whether winter persists or spring arrives early, the key is to remain flexible and responsive to what each season offers.

3. Harnessing the Power of Rituals

Rituals provide a sense of continuity and purpose, helping us navigate seasonal transitions with intention. Groundhog Day itself is a ritual that blends folklore, community, and humor to mark the shift from winter to spring. By creating personal or communal rituals, we can deepen our connection to the seasons and foster a sense of well-being.

- **Winter rituals:** Activities that promote rest and reflection, such as journaling, reading, or enjoying warm meals with loved ones.
- **Spring rituals:** Practices that encourage renewal and growth, such as gardening, decluttering, or setting new goals.
- **Summer rituals:** Celebrations of abundance and energy, such as outdoor gatherings, vacations, or pursuing creative projects.
- **Autumn rituals:** Acts of gratitude and preparation, such as preserving food, celebrating harvest festivals, or creating reflective lists.

These rituals ground us in the present while providing a framework for personal and communal growth, transforming seasonal changes into meaningful milestones.

4. Building Resilience During Seasonal Challenges

Each season presents unique challenges, from the harsh conditions of winter to the sweltering heat of summer. Thriving through these changes requires resilience—the ability to endure difficulties while maintaining a positive outlook.

- **Physical resilience:** Staying healthy by adapting diets, exercise routines, and self-care practices to the demands of each season. For example, boosting immunity during winter or staying active outdoors during summer.
- **Emotional resilience:** Developing coping strategies for seasonal mood shifts, such as using light therapy in winter or mindfulness practices during periods of high stress.
- **Community resilience:** Relying on social connections for support, whether through shared meals, collaborative projects, or simply spending time together.

Resilience allows us to face seasonal challenges with confidence and resourcefulness, transforming potential obstacles into opportunities for growth.

5. Aligning with Seasonal Opportunities

Each season offers unique opportunities for personal, professional, and spiritual growth. By aligning our actions and priorities with these opportunities, we can thrive in harmony with the natural world.

- **Winter opportunities:** Reflecting on the past year, setting long-term goals, and nurturing inner growth. Winter is an ideal time for learning, planning, and introspection.
- **Spring opportunities:** Launching new projects, pursuing creative endeavors, and cultivating relationships. Spring's energy is perfect for growth and exploration.
- **Summer opportunities:** Taking action, achieving milestones, and enjoying life's abundance. Summer encourages productivity, celebration, and outdoor activities.
- **Autumn opportunities:** Evaluating progress, expressing gratitude, and preparing for the future. Autumn invites reflection and the completion of important tasks.

By recognizing these opportunities, we can make intentional choices that align with the rhythm of each season, maximizing our potential for success and fulfillment.

6. Thriving Through Seasonal Transitions in Daily Life

Thriving through seasonal changes is not only about long-term strategies but also about small, everyday practices that enhance well-being and adaptability. These include:

- **Mindfulness practices:** Staying present and observing the subtle changes in nature, such as the lengthening of days or the first signs of spring blooms.
- **Seasonal self-care:** Adjusting routines to nurture physical and mental health, such as eating seasonal foods or prioritizing rest during busy periods.

- **Celebrating milestones:** Marking seasonal transitions with celebrations, whether it's a spring picnic, a summer barbecue, or an autumn harvest festival.

These practices help us stay connected to the present while preparing for what lies ahead, fostering a sense of continuity and balance.

7. Finding Joy in Every Season

Perhaps the most important lesson of thriving through seasonal changes is the ability to find joy and meaning in every phase. Each season, with its unique beauty and challenges, offers opportunities for wonder, gratitude, and connection. Groundhog Day, with its lighthearted celebration, reminds us to approach life's transitions with humor and optimism.

- **Winter joy:** Cozying up with loved ones, enjoying the stillness of snowy landscapes, or reflecting on personal growth.
- **Spring joy:** Watching flowers bloom, feeling the warmth of the sun, or embracing the excitement of new beginnings.
- **Summer joy:** Savoring long days, exploring the outdoors, or celebrating life's abundance.
- **Autumn joy:** Admiring vibrant foliage, harvesting fruits of labor, or cherishing moments of gratitude.

By cultivating an attitude of appreciation, we can transform seasonal transitions into opportunities for joy and inspiration.

Conclusion

Seasonal changes are a natural and inevitable part of life, offering endless opportunities for growth, reflection, and renewal. Thriving through these transitions requires adaptability, resilience, and the ability to align with the rhythms of nature. Groundhog Day serves as a poignant reminder of the beauty and significance of these cycles, inviting us to approach each season with intention and grace.

By embracing the lessons of the seasons, we can turn challenges into opportunities and find meaning in every phase of life. Whether waiting for spring, basking in summer, preparing in autumn, or reflecting in winter, the key to thriving lies in our ability to adapt, celebrate, and grow through the changes. In doing so, we not only honor the natural world but also unlock our potential to live fully and joyfully, no matter the season.

Appendix A: Seasonal Resilience Tips

This appendix provides practical and actionable tips to build resilience throughout the year, empowering you to navigate and thrive during each season's unique challenges. These strategies focus on mental, emotional, physical, and community resilience, ensuring a holistic approach to seasonal transitions. By adopting these tips, you can align your life with nature's cycles, maintain balance, and embrace the opportunities each season offers.

Winter Resilience Tips

Winter, often associated with cold temperatures and limited daylight, requires strategies to combat physical challenges, seasonal affective disorder (SAD), and a slower pace of life. Here's how to stay resilient during the darkest months:

1. Boost Your Immune System

- **Nutrition:** Focus on nutrient-rich, warming foods such as soups, stews, and herbal teas. Incorporate immune-boosting ingredients like garlic, ginger, citrus fruits, and leafy greens.
- **Hydration:** Stay hydrated, even if you feel less thirsty during cold weather.
- **Supplements:** Consider Vitamin D supplements to compensate for reduced sunlight exposure.

2. Combat Seasonal Affective Disorder

- **Light Therapy:** Use a light therapy box to mimic sunlight and boost your mood.
- **Daily Walks:** Spend time outdoors during daylight hours, even on cold days.
- **Social Connections:** Engage with family and friends to counteract feelings of isolation.

3. Stay Physically Active

- **Indoor Exercise:** Try yoga, pilates, or online workout classes to stay active without venturing outdoors.
- **Winter Sports:** Embrace seasonal activities like skiing, snowshoeing, or ice skating if weather permits.

4. Create a Cozy Environment

- **Hygge Practices:** Focus on creating warmth and comfort with candles, soft blankets, and warm beverages.
- **Decluttering:** Organize your space to create a calming atmosphere that supports relaxation and focus.

Spring Resilience Tips

Spring symbolizes renewal and growth but can also bring challenges like seasonal allergies, fluctuating weather, and the pressure to accomplish new goals. Here's how to thrive during spring:

1. Embrace Fresh Starts

- **Set New Goals:** Use spring's energy to revisit your resolutions and set achievable milestones.
- **Declutter:** Spring cleaning isn't just physical—declutter your digital life, relationships, and commitments.

2. Manage Seasonal Allergies

- **Allergy Prevention:** Use air purifiers, wash bedding frequently, and stay indoors during peak pollen times.
- **Hydration:** Drink plenty of water to alleviate allergy symptoms and keep your body functioning optimally.
- **Natural Remedies:** Try local honey, herbal teas, or steam inhalation to soothe symptoms.

3. Reconnect with Nature

- **Gardening:** Plant flowers, vegetables, or herbs to connect with the earth and enjoy the therapeutic benefits of gardening.
- **Outdoor Activities:** Hike, bike, or take leisurely walks to soak up spring's beauty and energy.

4. Revitalize Your Routine

- **Healthy Eating:** Incorporate fresh, seasonal produce like asparagus, spinach, and strawberries into your meals.

- **Physical Activity:** Increase outdoor activities as the weather improves to boost energy and mood.

Summer Resilience Tips

Summer is a season of abundance and high energy but can also bring heat, over-scheduling, and fatigue. These tips help you stay balanced and resilient:

1. Stay Cool and Hydrated

- **Hydration:** Drink water consistently, and consider infused waters with fruit or herbs for variety.
- **Cooling Foods:** Incorporate water-rich foods like cucumbers, watermelon, and leafy greens.
- **Shade and Sunscreen:** Protect yourself from the sun with hats, sunglasses, and sunscreen.

2. Balance Activity and Rest

- **Pacing:** Don't overcommit; balance social engagements with time for relaxation.
- **Evening Wind-Downs:** Use cooler evenings to recharge with calming activities like reading or stargazing.

3. Maximize Outdoor Opportunities

- **Recreational Activities:** Explore outdoor hobbies like camping, paddleboarding, or picnicking.
- **Nature Appreciation:** Practice mindfulness in nature by observing sunsets, beaches, or local parks.

4. Practice Gratitude

- **Seasonal Journaling:** Reflect on what you're grateful for during summer, such as time with loved ones or simple pleasures like ice cream on a hot day.

Autumn Resilience Tips

Autumn's themes of harvest and preparation come with shorter days, cooler temperatures, and increased workloads. Here's how to thrive during this transitional season:

1. Prepare for Winter

- **Stock Supplies:** Organize your pantry and ensure you have essentials like warm clothing and emergency kits.
- **Maintenance:** Winterize your home and vehicle to prepare for colder months.

2. Celebrate the Harvest

- **Seasonal Foods:** Enjoy autumn's bounty with dishes featuring pumpkins, squash, apples, and root vegetables.
- **Preservation:** Try canning, freezing, or drying seasonal produce to enjoy throughout winter.

3. Create a Cozy Ambiance

- **Warm Decor:** Incorporate autumnal colors and textures like flannel throws and scented candles into your living space.
- **Seasonal Rituals:** Celebrate with traditions like apple picking, carving pumpkins, or hosting harvest-themed dinners.

4. Stay Grounded Amid Change

- **Mindfulness Practices:** Reflect on your achievements and set intentions for the remainder of the year.
- **Exercise Routine:** Adjust your physical activity to suit cooler weather, such as brisk walks or indoor yoga.

General Tips for Year-Round Resilience
1. Build a Seasonal Self-Care Plan

- Create a personalized self-care checklist for each season to ensure you prioritize your mental and physical health.

2. Maintain Social Connections

- Stay engaged with loved ones, whether through regular gatherings, video calls, or shared activities that celebrate the season.

3. Practice Gratitude

- Keep a gratitude journal to reflect on the unique gifts each season brings, from winter's stillness to summer's vibrancy.

4. Embrace Seasonal Learning

- Read books, watch documentaries, or take workshops that deepen your understanding of each season's cultural and natural significance.

5. Reevaluate Goals Quarterly

- Use the changing seasons as a natural checkpoint to assess and adjust your personal, professional, and creative goals.

Conclusion

Resilience is not about resisting change but thriving within it. By embracing the unique challenges and opportunities each season presents, you can cultivate a balanced and fulfilling life. These seasonal resilience tips provide practical ways to align with nature's rhythms, ensuring that you remain grounded, adaptable, and ready to flourish no matter the time of year.

Message from the Author:

I hope you enjoyed this book, I love astrology and knew there was not a book such as this out on the shelf. I love metaphysical items as well. Please check out my other books:

-Life of Government Benefits
-My life of Hell
-My life with Hydrocephalus
-Red Sky
-World Domination:Woman's rule
-World Domination:Woman's Rule 2: The War
-Life and Banishment of Apophis: book 1
-The Kidney Friendly Diet
-The Ultimate Hemp Cookbook
-Creating a Dispensary(legally)
-Cleanliness throughout life: the importance of showering from childhood to adulthood.
-Strong Roots: The Risks of Overcoddling children
-Hemp Horoscopes: Cosmic Insights and Earthly Healing
- Celestial Hemp Navigating the Zodiac: Through the Green Cosmos
-Astrological Hemp: Aligning The Stars with Earth's Ancient Herb
-The Astrological Guide to Hemp: Stars, Signs, and Sacred Leaves
-Green Growth: Innovative Marketing Strategies for your Hemp Products and Dispensary
-Cosmic Cannabis
-Astrological Munchies
-Henry The Hemp
-Zodiacal Roots: The Astrological Soul Of Hemp
- **Green Constellations: Intersection of Hemp and Zodiac**
-Hemp in The Houses: An astrological Adventure Through The Cannabis Galaxy
-Galactic Ganja Guide
Heavenly Hemp

Zodiac Leaves
Doctor Who Astrology
Cannastrology
Stellar Satvias and Cosmic Indicas
<u>Celestial Cannabis: A Zodiac Journey</u>
AstroHerbology: The Sky and The Soil: Volume 1
AstroHerbology:Celestial Cannabis:Volume 2
Cosmic Cannabis Cultivation
The Starry Guide to Herbal Harmony: Volume 1
The Starry Guide to Herbal Harmony: Cannabis Universe: Volume 2

Yugioh Astrology: Astrological Guide to Deck, Duels and more
Nightmare Mansion: Echoes of The Abyss
Nightmare Mansion 2: Legacy of Shadows
Nightmare Mansion 3: Shadows of the Forgotten
Nightmare Mansion 4: Echoes of the Damned
The Life and Banishment of Apophis: Book 2
Nightmare Mansion: Halls of Despair
<u>Healing with Herb: Cannabis and Hydrocephalus</u>
<u>Planetary Pot: Aligning with Astrological Herbs: Volume 1</u>
Fast Track to Freedom: 30 Days to Financial Independence Using AI, Assets, and Agile Hustles
<u>Cosmic Hemp Pathways</u>
How to Become Financially Free in 30 Days: 10,000 Paths to Prosperity
Zodiacal Herbage: Astrological Insights: Volume 1
Nightmare Mansion: Whispers in the Walls
The Daleks Invade Atlantis
Henry the hemp and Hydrocephalus

10X The Kidney Friendly Diet
Cannabis Universe: Adult coloring book
Hemp Astrology: The Healing Power of the Stars

Zodiacal Herbage: Astrological Insights: Cannabis Universe: Volume 2

Planetary Pot: Aligning with Astrological Herbs: Cannabis Universes: Volume 2

Doctor Who Meets the Replicators and SG-1: The Ultimate Battle for Survival

Nightmare Mansion: Curse of the Blood Moon

The Celestial Stoner: A Guide to the Zodiac

Cosmic Pleasures: Sex Toy Astrology for Every Sign

Hydrocephalus Astrology: Navigating the Stars and Healing Waters

Lapis and the Mischievous Chocolate Bar

Celestial Positions: Sexual Astrology for Every Sign

Apophis's Shadow Work Journal: : A Journey of Self-Discovery and Healing

Kinky Cosmos: Sexual Kink Astrology for Every Sign

Digital Cosmos: The Astrological Digimon Compendium

Stellar Seeds: The Cosmic Guide to Growing with Astrology

Apophis's Daily Gratitude Journal

Cat Astrology: Feline Mysteries of the Cosmos

The Cosmic Kama Sutra: An Astrological Guide to Sexual Positions

Unleash Your Potential: A Guided Journal Powered by AI Insights

Whispers of the Enchanted Grove

Cosmic Pleasures: An Astrological Guide to Sexual Kinks

369, 12 Manifestation Journal

Whisper of the nocturne journal(blank journal for writing or drawing)

The Boogey Book

Locked In Reflection: A Chastity Journey Through Locktober
Generating Wealth Quickly:
How to Generate $100,000 in 24 Hours
Star Magic: Harness the Power of the Universe
The Flatulence Chronicles: A Fart Journal for Self-Discovery
The Doctor and The Death Moth
Seize the Day: A Personal Seizure Tracking Journal
The Ultimate Boogeyman Safari: A Journey into the Boogie World and Beyond

Whispers of Samhain: 1,000 Spells of Love, Luck, and Lunar Magic: Samhain Spell Book

Apophis's guides:

Witch's Spellbook Crafting Guide for Halloween

Frost & Flame: The Enchanted Yule Grimoire of 1000 Winter Spells

The Ultimate Boogey Goo Guide & Spooky Activities for Halloween Fun

Harmony of the Scales: A Libra's Spellcraft for Balance and Beauty
The Enchanted Advent: 36 Days of Christmas Wonders

Nightmare Mansion: The Labyrinth of Screams

Harvest of Enchantment: 1,000 Spells of Gratitude, Love, and Fortune for Thanksgiving
The Boogey Chronicles: A Journal of Nightly Encounters and Shadowy Secrets
The 12 Days of Financial Freedom: A Step-by-Step Christmas Countdown to Transform Your Finances
Sigil of the Eternal Spiral Blank Journal
A Christmas Feast: Timeless Recipes for Every Meal
Holiday Stress-Free Solutions: A Survival Guide to Thriving During the Festive Season
Yu-Gi-Oh! Holiday Gifting Mastery: The Ultimate Guide for Fans and Newcomers Alike

Holiday Harmony: A Hydrocephalus Survival Guide for the Festive Season

Celestial Craft: The Witch's Almanac for 2025 – A Cosmic Guide to Manifestations, Moons, and Mystical Events

Doctor Who: The Toymaker's Winter Wonderland

Tulsa King Unveiled: A Thrilling Guide to Stallone's Mafia Masterpiece

Pendulum Craft: A Complete Guide to Crafting and Using Personalized Divination Tools

Nightmare Mansion: Santa's Eternal Eve

Starlight Noel: A Cosmic Journey through Christmas Mysteries

The Dark Architect: Unlocking the Blueprint of Existence

Surviving the Embrace: The Ultimate Guide to Encounters with The Hugging Molly

The Enchanted Codex: Secrets of the Craft for Witches, Wiccans, and Pagans

Harvest of Gratitude: A Complete Thanksgiving Guide

Yuletide Essentials: A Complete Guide to an Authentic and Magical Christmas

Celestial Smokes: A Cosmic Guide to Cigars and Astrology

Living in Balance: A Comprehensive Survival Guide to Thriving with Diabetes Insipidus

Cosmic Symbiosis: The Venom Zodiac Chronicles

The Cursed Paw of Ambition

Cosmic Symbiosis: The Astrological Venom Journal

Celestial Wonders Unfold: A Stargazer's Guide to the Cosmos (2024-2029)

The Ultimate Black Friday Prepper's Guide: Mastering Shopping Strategies and Savings

Cosmic Sales: The Astrological Guide to Black Friday Shopping

Legends of the Corn Mother and Other Harvest Myths

Whispers of the Harvest: The Corn Mother's Journal

The Evergreen Spellbook

The Doctor Meets the Boogeyman
The White Witch of Rose Hall's SpellBook
The Gingerbread Golem's Shadow: A Study in Sweet Darkness
The Gingerbread Golem Codex: An Academic Exploration of Sweet Myths
The Gingerbread Golem Grimoire: Sweet Magicks and Spells for the Festive Witch
The Curse of the Gingerbread Golem
10-minute Christmas Crafts for kids
Christmas Crisis Solutions: The Ultimate Last-Minute Survival Guide
Gingerbread Golem Recipes: Holiday Treats with a Magical Twist
The Infinite Key: Unlocking Mystical Secrets of the Ages
Enchanted Yule: A Wiccan and Pagan Guide to a Magical and Memorable Season
Dinosaurs of Power: Unlocking Ancient Magick
Astro-Dinos: The Cosmic Guide to Prehistoric Wisdom
Gallifrey's Yule Logs: A Festive Doctor Who Cookbook
The Dino Grimoire: Secrets of Prehistoric Magick
The Gift They Never Knew They Needed
The Gingerbread Golem's Culinary Alchemy: Enchanting Recipes for a Sweetly Dark Feast
A Time Lord Christmas: Holiday Adventures with the Doctor
Krampusproofing Your Home: Defensive Strategies for Yule
Silent Frights: A Collection of Christmas Creepypastas to Chill Your Bones
Santa Raptor's Jolly Carnage: A Dino-Claus Christmas Tale
Prehistoric Palettes: A Dino Wicca Coloring Journey
The Christmas Wishkeeper Chronicles
The Starlight Sleigh: A Holiday Journey
Elf Secrets: The True Magic of the North Pole
Candy Cane Conjurations
Cooking with Kids: Recipes Under 20 Minutes

Doctor Who: The TARDIS Confiscation
The Anxiety First Aid Kit: Quick Tools to Calm Your Mind
Frosty Whispers: A Winter's Tale
The Infinite Key: Unlocking the Secrets to Prosperity, Resilience, and Purpose
The Grasping Void: Why You'll Regret This Purchase
Astrology for Busy Bees: Star Signs Simplified
The Instant Focus Formula: Cut Through the Noise
The Secret Language of Colors: Unlocking the Emotional Codes
Sacred Fossil Chronicles: Blank Journal
The Christmas Cottage Miracle
Feeding Frenzy: Graboid-Inspired Recipes
Manifest in Minutes: The Quick Law of Attraction Guide
The Symbiote Chronicles: Doctor Who's Venomous Journey
Think Tiny, Grow Big: The Minimalist Mindset
The Energy Key: Unlocking Limitless Motivation
New Year, New Magic: Manifesting Your Best Year Yet
Unstoppable You: Mastering Confidence in Minutes
Infinite Energy: The Secret to Never Feeling Drained
Lightning Focus: Mastering the Art of Productivity in a Distracted World
Saturnalia Manifestation Magick: A Guide to Unlocking Abundance During the Solstice
Graboids and Garland: The Ultimate Tremors-Themed Christmas Guide
12 Nights of Holiday Magic
The Power of Pause: 60-Second Mindfulness Practices
The Quick Reset: How to Reclaim Your Life After Burnout
The Shadow Eater: A Tale of Despair and Survival
The Micro-Mastery Method: Transform Your Skills in Just Minutes a Day
Reclaiming Time: How to Live More by Doing Less
Chronovore: The Eternal Nexus

The Mind Reset: Unlocking Your Inner Peace in a Chaotic World
Confidence Code: Building Unshakable Self-Belief
Baby the Vampire Terrier
Baby the Vampire Terrier's Christmas Adventure
Celestial Streams: The Content Creator's Astrology Manual
The Wealth Whisperer: Unlocking Abundance with Everyday Actions
The Energy Equation: Maximize Your Output Without Burning Out
The Happiness Algorithm: Science-Backed Steps to Joyful Living
Stress-Free Success: Achieving Goals Without Anxiety
Mindful Wealth: The New Blueprint for Financial Freedom
The Festive Flavors of New Year: A Culinary Celebration
The Master's Gambit: Keys of Eternal Power
Shadowed Secrets: Groundhog Day Mysteries
Beneath the Burrow: Lessons from the Groundhog
Spring's Whispers: The Groundhog's Prediction
The Limitless Mindset: Unlock Your Untapped Potential
The Focus Funnel: How to Cut Through Chaos and Get Results
Bold Moves: Building Courage to Live on Your Terms
The Daily Shift: Simple Practices for Lasting Transformation
The Quarter-Life Reset: Thriving in Your 20s and 30s
The Art of Shadowplay: Building Your Own Personal Myth
The Eternal Loop: Finding Purpose in Repetition
Burrowing Wisdom: Life Lessons from the Groundhog
Shadow Work: A Groundhog Day Perspective
Love in Bloom: 5-Minute Romantic Gestures
The Shadowspell Codex: Secrets of Forbidden Magick
The Burnout Cure: Finding Balance in a Busy World
The Groundhog Prophecy: Unlocking Seasonal Secrets
Nog Tales: The Spirited History of Eggnog
Six More Weeks: Embracing Seasonal Transitions
The Lumivian Chronicles: Fragments of the Fifth Dimension

Money on Your Mind: A Beginner's Guide to Wealth
The Focus Fix: Breaking Through Distraction
January's Spirit Keepers: Mystical Protectors of the Cold
Creativity Unchained: Unlocking Your Wildest Ideas in 2025
Manifestation Mastery: 365 Days to Rewrite Your Reality
The Groundhog's Mirror: Reflecting on Change
The Weeping Angels' Christmas Curse
Burrowed in Time: A Groundhog Day Journey
Heartbeats: Poems to Share with Your Valentine
Dino Wicca: The Sacred Grimoire of Prehistoric Magick
Courage of the Pride: Finding Your Inner Roar
The Lion's Leap: Bold Moves for Big Results
Healthy Hustle: Achieving Without Overworking
Practical Manifesting: Turning Dreams into Reality in 2025
Jurassic Pharaohs: Unlocking the Magick of Ancient Egypt and Dino Wicca
The Happiness Equation: Small Changes for Big Joy
The Confidence Compass: Finding Your Inner Strength
Whispers in the Hollow: Tales of the Forgotten Beasts
Echoes from the Hollow: The Return of Forgotten Beasts
The Hollow Ascendant: The Rise of the Forgotten Beasts
The Relationship Reset: Building Better Connections
Mastering the Morning: How to Win the Day Before 8 AM
The Shadow's Dance: Groundhog Day Symbolism
Cupid's Kitchen: Quick Valentine's Day Recipes
Valentine's Day on a Budget: Love Without Breaking the Bank
Astrocraft: Aligning the Stars in the World of Minecraft
Forecasting Life: Groundhog Day Reflections

Bleeding Hearts: Twisted Tales of Valentine's Terror

Herbal Smoke Revolution: The Ultimate Guide to Nature's Cigarette Alternative

Winter's Wrath: The Complete Survival Blueprint for Extreme Freezes.

The Groundhog's Shadow: A Tale of Seasons
Burrowed Insights: Wisdom from the Groundhog
Sensual Strings: The Art of Erotic Bondage
Whispered Flames: Unlocking the Power of Fire Play
Forgotten Shadows: A Guide to Cryptids Lost to Time
Six Weeks of Secrets: Groundhog Day's Hidden Messages
Shadows and Cycles: Groundhog Day Reflections
The Art of Love Letters: Crafting the Perfect Message
Romantic Getaways at Home: Turning Your Space into Paradise
Purrfect Brews: A Cat Lover's Guide to Coffee and Companionship
The Groundhog's Wisdom: Timeless Lessons for Modern Life
The Shadow Oracle: Groundhog Day as a Predictor
Emerging from the Burrow: A Journey of Renewal
The Language of Love: Learning Your Partner's Love Style
Authorpreneur: The Ultimate Blueprint for Writing, Publishing, and Thriving as an Author

If you want solar for your home go here: https://www.harborsolar.live/apophisenterprises/

Get Some Tarot cards: https://www.makeplayingcards.com/sell/apophis-occult-shop

Get some shirts: https://www.bonfire.com/store/apophis-shirt-emporium/

Instagrams:
@apophis_enterprises,
@apophisbookemporium,
@apophisscardshop
Twitter: @apophisenterpr1
Tiktok:@apophisenterprise
Youtube: @sg1fan23477, @FiresideRetreatKingdom
Hive: @sg1fan23477
CheeLee: @SG1fan23477

Podcast: Apophis Chat Zone: https://open.spotify.com/show/5zXbrCLEV2xzCp8ybrfHsk?si=fb4d4fdbdce44dec

Newsletter: https://apophiss-newsletter-27c897.beehiiv.com/

If you want to support me or see posts of other projects that I have come over to: **buymeacoffee.com/mpetchinskg**

I post there daily several times a day

Get your Dinowicca or Christmas themed digital products, especially Santa Raptor songs and other musics. Here: **https://sg1fan23477.gumroad.com**

Apophis Yuletide Digital has not only digital Christmas items, but it will have all things with Dinowicca as well as other Digital products.

www.ingramcontent.com/pod-product-compliance
Ingram Content Group UK Ltd.
Pitfield, Milton Keynes, MK11 3LW, UK
UKHW021015050225
454710UK00012B/675